A YEAR IN COLOR

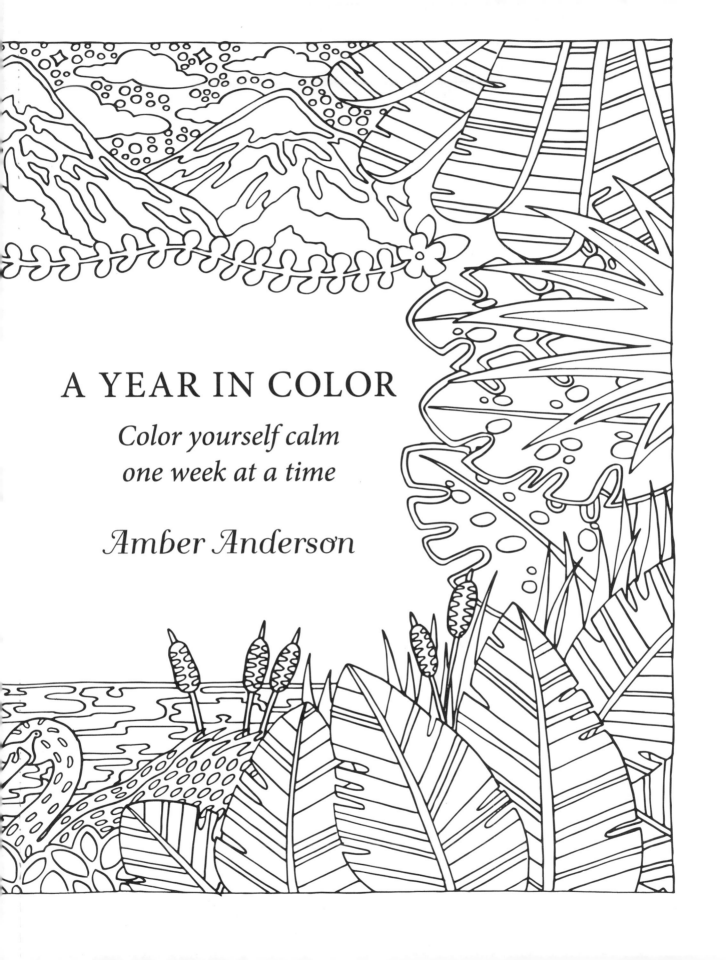

A YEAR IN COLOR

Color yourself calm
one week at a time

Amber Anderson

A YEAR IN COLOR

Pegasus Books Ltd.
148 W 37th Street, 13th Floor
New York, NY 10018

First Pegasus Books edition January 2017

ISBN: 978-1-68177-360-5

10 9 8 7 6 5 4 3 2 1

Printed in the United States of America
Distributed by W. W. Norton & Company, Inc.

Do you ever wish you had just a bit more time? Do you feel like you're often running late, or are surprised that the year is suddenly half-gone even though it seems like you were celebrating the new year last week? Time passing can be stressful, but it can be the antidote to stress as well, if we just remember to take a little of it for ourselves: by reflecting on the cycle of the seasons and the passing of the year, we can see how there is always enough time—and the right time—for the really important things, and for simple pastimes like coloring.

Coloring has been shown to reduce stress and improve our day-to-day lives by giving us a moment to relax, reflect and focus on something creative and personal. By keeping this beautiful book with you throughout the year, reflecting on the quotations and affirmations inside, and devoting a little time to it each week, you'll find you have more time to appreciate the things that matter.

JANUARY
Week 1

The most certain way to succeed
is always to try just one more time.

—THOMAS EDISON

JANUARY
Week 2

Hope is a waking dream.

—ARISTOTLE

JANUARY
Week 3

I ask not for any crown
But that which all may win;
Nor try to conquer any world
Except the one within.

—LOUISA MAY ALCOTT

JANUARY
Week 4

Few people know how to take a walk.
The qualifications are endurance, plain
clothes, old shoes, an eye for nature, good
humour, vast curiosity, good speech,
good silence and nothing too much.

—RALPH WALDO EMERSON

FEBRUARY
Week 5

He who is best prepared can best
serve his moment of inspiration.
—SAMUEL TAYLOR COLERIDGE

FEBRUARY

Week 6

You make a living by what you get;
you make a life by what you give.

—WINSTON CHURCHILL

FEBRUARY
Week 7

Three things cannot be hidden:
the sun, the moon, and the truth.

—BUDDHA

FEBRUARY
Week 8

We have all a better guide in ourselves,
if we would attend to it, than any other
person can be.

—JANE AUSTEN

A lake is the landscape's most beautiful
and expressive feature. It is Earth's eye;
looking into which the beholder measures
the depth of his own nature.

—HENRY DAVID THOREAU

MARCH
Week 10

Spiderwebs united can bind a lion.
                    —AFRICAN PROVERB

MARCH
Week 11

Be still, sad heart! and cease repining;
Behind the clouds is the sun still shining.
                    —HENRY WADSWORTH LONGFELLOW

MARCH
Week 12

While you are proclaiming peace with
your lips, be careful to have it even
more fully in your heart.

—ST. FRANCIS OF ASSISI

MARCH–APRIL
Week 13

A loving heart is the truest wisdom.
—CHARLES DICKENS

APRIL
Week 14

You only live once, but if you do it right, once is enough.

—MAE WEST

APRIL
Week 15

Don't walk behind me; I may not lead.
Don't walk in front of me; I may not follow.
Just walk beside me and be my friend.
                                        —ALBERT CAMUS

APRIL
Week 16

To be yourself in a world that is constantly trying to make you something else is the greatest accomplishment.

—RALPH WALDO EMERSON

APRIL–MAY
Week 17

Not all of us can do great things. But we
can do small things with great love.

—MOTHER TERESA

MAY

Week 18

Being deeply loved by someone gives you strength, while loving someone deeply gives you courage.

—LAO TZU

MAY
Week 19

Life is like riding a bicycle. To keep your balance, you must keep moving.

—ALBERT EINSTEIN

MAY
Week 20

Admitting you do not know everything
shows more wisdom than believing you
have all the answers.

—ANONYMOUS

MAY
Week 21

My dear friend, clear your mind of can't.

—SAMUEL JOHNSON

The will to win, the desire to succeed,
the urge to reach your full potential . . .
these are the keys that will unlock the door
to personal excellence.

—CONFUCIUS

JUNE
Week 23

Do one thing every day that scares you.
—ELEANOR ROOSEVELT

JUNE
Week 24

You have power over your mind—not
outside events. Realize this, and you will
find strength.

—MARCUS AURELIUS

JUNE
Week 25

Like madness is the glory of life.
—WILLIAM SHAKESPEARE

JUNE–JULY

Week 26

To create a little flower is the labour of ages.

—WILLIAM BLAKE

JULY

Week 27

Be yourself, everyone else is already taken.

—OSCAR WILDE

JULY
Week 28

Every limit is a beginning as well as
an ending.

—GEORGE ELIOT

JULY
Week 29

Love should be unconditional; when you give it in this way you will receive it back in abundance.

—ANONYMOUS

JULY
Week 30

Time stays long enough for anyone
who will use it.

—LEONARDO DA VINCI

AUGUST
Week 31

Life without love is like a tree without blossoms or fruit.

—KAHLIL GIBRAN

AUGUST
Week 32

Try not to become a man of success,
but rather try to become a man of value.

—ALBERT EINSTEIN

AUGUST
Week 33

Only deeds speak. Words are nothing.

—AFRICAN PROVERB

AUGUST
Week 34

The greatest prayer is patience.

—BUDDHA

AUGUST–SEPTEMBER
Week 35

If you tell the truth, you don't have to
remember anything.

—MARK TWAIN

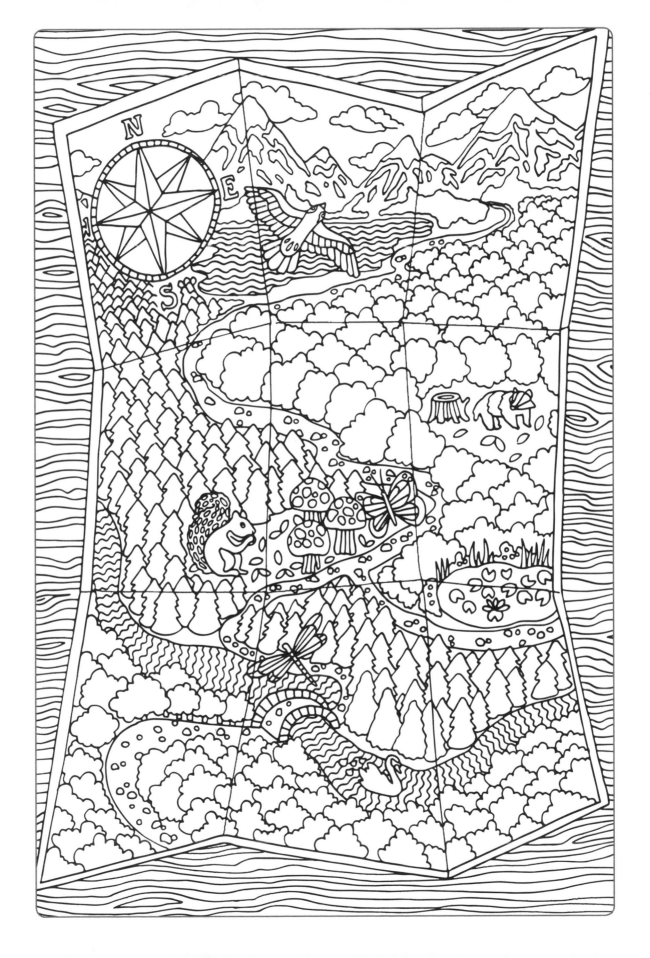

SEPTEMBER

Week 36

The fool doth think he is wise, but the wise
man knows himself to be a fool.

—WILLIAM SHAKESPEARE

SEPTEMBER
Week 37

If you judge people, you have no time
to love them.

—MOTHER TERESA

SEPTEMBER
Week 38

Folks are usually about as happy as they
make their minds up to be.

—ABRAHAM LINCOLN

Be a master of mind, rather than mastered
by mind.

—ZEN SAYING

OCTOBER
Week 40

Be the change that you wish to see in the world.

—MAHATMA GANDHI

OCTOBER
Week 41

There is no charm equal to tenderness of heart.

—JANE AUSTEN

OCTOBER
Week 42

As a bee gathering nectar does not harm
or disturb the colour and fragrance of
the flower; so do the wise move through
the world.

—BUDDHA

OCTOBER

Week 43

My true religion is kindness.

—DALAI LAMA

OCTOBER–NOVEMBER

Week 44

The only way to have a friend is to be one.
—RALPH WALDO EMERSON

NOVEMBER
Week 45

Happy is the man who has broken the
chains which hurt the mind, and has given
up worrying once and for all.

—OVID

NOVEMBER

Week 46

I confess I do not know why, but looking at
the stars always makes me dream.

—VINCENT VAN GOGH

NOVEMBER
Week 47

Correction does much, but encouragement
does more.

—JOHANN WOLFGANG VON GOETHE

Life is 10 percent what happens to you and 90 percent how you react to it.

DECEMBER
Week 49

No kind action ever stops with itself. The greatest work that kindness does to others is that it makes them kind themselves.

—AMELIA EARHART

DECEMBER
Week 50

Any man that walks the mead
In bud, or blade, or bloom, may find
A meaning suited to his mind.

—ALFRED TENNYSON

DECEMBER
Week 51

Share the kindness that's in your soul.
Even the smallest acts of generosity can
bring great joy to yourself and others.

—ANONYMOUS

DECEMBER

Week 52

Success is not final, failure is not fatal:
it is the courage to continue that counts.

—WINSTON CHURCHILL